Many Blessings!

Gary Bower

2020

The ABCs of

GOD

A Family Devotional Exploring 26 of God's Attributes

by Gary Bower

Storybook Meadow Publishing
Traverse City, Michigan

To Jan

my dear wife of 40 years,
whose unwavering trust in God
and steady devotion to me at my bedside
helped me to look beyond my circumstances
and write much of this book during a time of illness.

The photography in this book comes from two sources:
    — Pixabay.com public domain photographs released under Creative Commons CC0, which the author has gratefully used in careful compliance with their terms, applicable laws, rules, and regulations.
    — Personal photographs taken by the author, his family members, and friends, used by permission and with appreciation.

www.GaryBower.com

ISBN-13: 978-1-7321629-0-7

Printed and bound in the United States of America.

Contents

What Others Are Saying about *"The ABCs of God"*

"Can a single book help teach your kids the ABCs and also impart deep theological truth? Gary Bower proves that it's possible in **The ABCs of God***. With engaging text and colorful photos throughout, this book will help you explore God's attributes and character through each letter of the alphabet. This is a great resource for busy moms and dads!"*

— Dr. Greg Smalley
Vice President, Marriage and Family Formation, Focus on the Family

"Chasing a deeper awareness of the magnificent realities of God's nature is a life-transforming quest that will inspire us to worship more freely and to love Him more deeply. This quest will never be boring, since exploring the unfathomable depths of God's character is a lifelong journey of discovery. In **The ABCs of God***, Gary Bower has done an excellent job of helping us start this quest from the limited dimensions of our small, fleeting lives into the awesome realm of the rich and endless glory of our God!"*

— Dr. Joseph Stowell
President, Cornerstone University & Grand Rapids Theological Seminary
and author of 30 books

"I believe we are born with a desire to know God deeply — to understand who He is and how we fit into His ultimate plan. **The ABCs of God** *is a family-friendly devotional that guides parents and children along the path to exploring the depth of God's attributes and character, bringing readers into a close and loving relationship with our heavenly Father. With Bible verses sprinkled on scenic pages, rhythmic poetry, thoughts of reflection, and heartfelt prayers, Gary Bower has created a powerful resource that belongs in every home."*

— Crystal Bowman
Bestselling author of 100 children's books, including **Our Daily Bread for Kids**

"It was my privilege to teach theology to Gary Bower at Fort Wayne Bible College back in the 1970s. One whole semester was devoted to the study of God and His attributes. What a blessing it is for me to see one of my students passing on these great truths to younger generations! I recommend **The ABCs of God** *to parents, grandparents, teachers, and all others who want to introduce God's character to children in an interesting and helpful manner."*

— Dr. Wesley L. Gerig
Professor of Bible, Theology, and Biblical Languages for 51 years,
Fort Wayne Bible College and Taylor University Fort Wayne

*"***The ABCs of God** *is a fantastic book for both children and adults with its focused themes, beautiful graphics, and powerful message. It is a wonderful tool to teach children who God is and what God has done. Gary Bower has developed a great format for families and churches to thank God in prayer, from A to Z!"*

— Rev. Craig Trierweiler
Senior Pastor, New Hope Community Church, Williamsburg, Michigan

---

Acknowledgements

I am grateful for the family members, friends, teachers, coaches, camp counselors, pastors, and authors who have "salted my oats" and made me thirsty to know God better. In particular, I want to acknowledge two from whom I have drawn significant inspiration that eventually led to the writing of this book:

A.W. Tozer, whose eloquent writings, especially *The Knowledge of the Holy* and *The Pursuit of God*, took my spirit to new heights and my mind to broader vistas while I was in my teen years.

Dr. Wesley Gerig, my theology professor at Fort Wayne Bible College, who urged his students to search the Scriptures for divine attributes by which God has described Himself. I hope that Dr. Wes (who always asked for "nouns, please") will pardon my usage of so many predicate adjectives.

Introduction

My earliest memory of attempting to tackle the "who is God?" question is as a three-year-old in a church nursery. I got into a fairly intense theological "debate" with another little boy about whether God and Jesus were the same person or two distinct individuals. I can't recall which side of the issue I was arguing, but I remember it ending in a frustrating stalemate. Unfortunately, that discussion – like too much religious talk today – was more combative than inspiring. But it sparked in my confused little mind a curiosity about my Maker – a fascination that burned ever brighter as time passed. As a teen I devoured books that talked about the Divine Nature, and in my college years grand terms like *omnipotence, omnipresence, omniscience, immutability, transcendence,* and *infinitude* stretched my mind and fueled stimulating conversations on campus.

Decades later, during an illness that had me bedridden for many weeks, I found strength in trusting that my condition might serve an eternal purpose. I tried to recall times when God had been faithful to my family in difficult circumstances. I clung stubbornly to my belief that God is good, no matter what. One day I noticed the sequence of E-F-G: eternal, faithful, good. Suddenly, my mind was on a mission that distracted me from the physical pain. My spirit eagerly climbed on board as I wrote the poetry contained in this book.

My college days are long past, and many children and grandchildren have entered my world. They help me remember that, while splendiferous terminology has its place, there is also value in bending the branches a little lower so the fruit can be picked more easily. In **The ABCs of God** I have replaced big words with simpler synonyms, such as *Almighty* for *Omnipotent*, and *Unchanging* instead of *Immutable*. Of course, some letters could stand for many attributes (for example, the letter "G" also could stand for *Gracious, Giving, Glorious*, etc.), so I have tried to assign words to letters in a way that would avoid being redundant with some characteristics and remiss with others.

May this simple alphabet book stir a hunger in you to know God a little bit better.

— *Gary Bower*

How To Use This Book

The ABCs of God can be used effectively in a number of settings:

• **FAMILY:** The easy-to-read rhymes, graphics, and short readings appeal to all ages.
• **GROUP:** The Biblical concepts with supporting verses will stimulate great discussions.
• **INDIVIDUAL:** It offers a personal devotional opportunity to grow closer to God.

To get the most out of **The ABCs of God**:

1. Read the **"God is..."** characteristic first, followed by the 10-line poem.
2. Look up the Bible verses, reading them in context to shed even more light on that particular Biblical truth.
3. Take **"A Closer Look"** - This offers a few additional thoughts for consideration and further study.
4. **"Talk to God"** - This is only a suggested guide to help you pray. Your Heavenly Father, of course, is interested in hearing you express whatever is on **your** heart.

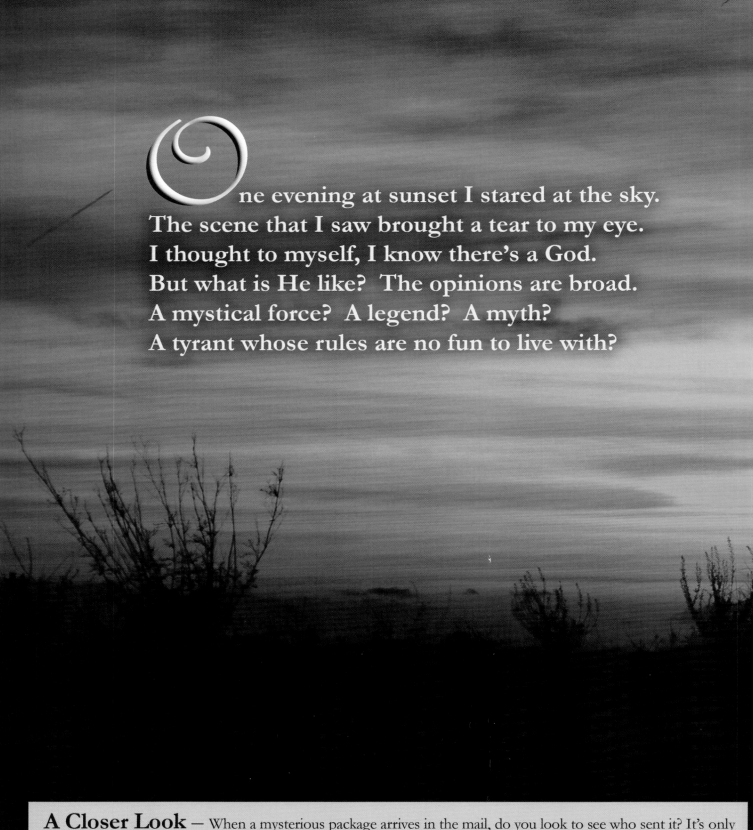

One evening at sunset I stared at the sky.
The scene that I saw brought a tear to my eye.
I thought to myself, I know there's a God.
But what is He like? The opinions are broad.
A mystical force? A legend? A myth?
A tyrant whose rules are no fun to live with?

A Closer Look — When a mysterious package arrives in the mail, do you look to see who sent it? It's only natural to wonder where things come from. People research their family tree, going back generations to learn about their history. Scientists are curious about the origin of the universe. Of course, the vast majority of people believe that it all came from God. The obvious and overwhelming evidence for His existence is all around them, so, naturally, they want to know more about their Maker. It is reasonable to believe that a God capable of designing an intelligent being like you — someone whose mind has the capacity to think thoughts about God — would also be perfectly capable of revealing Himself to you. There is no greater quest than pursuing the truth about God. The Bible promises that if you seek God with all your heart, He will let you find Him (Jeremiah 29:13).

Talk to God — *"God, I don't have to look far to see evidence of You. The fact that I am aware of myself and can perceive my surroundings shows me that I am far more than a collection of molecules. I can sense things, think thoughts, ask questions, and feel desire. I believe that You designed me with these abilities and many others, and I want to know more about who You are."*

Thank God for your curiosity about Him, for the ability to reason, and the desire to explore who He is.

To answer my questions, where should I go?
Straight to the Source, of course! He ought to know!
I reached for the Bible that sat on my shelf
to see just what God had to say for Himself.

Closer Look — The Bible is like no other book in the history of the world. Although it is thousands of [year]s old, millions and millions of people still find it relevant and life-changing today. All across the globe, in [over] three-thousand languages, young and old draw their strength, courage, hope, and wisdom from it every day. [The]y know they can trust what it says. It is a true historical record of our world that has stood the test of time with [astou]nding archeological, scientific, and prophetic accuracy. Over and over within its pages, the Bible claims to be [the] Word of God. No wonder it speaks so powerfully to the human heart! Many brave men and women have given [their] lives to proclaim it and preserve it when kings and emperors have tried to destroy it. Even when governments [try to] silence it, the Bible keeps on changing lives because "the Word of the Lord endures forever" (1 Peter 1:25).

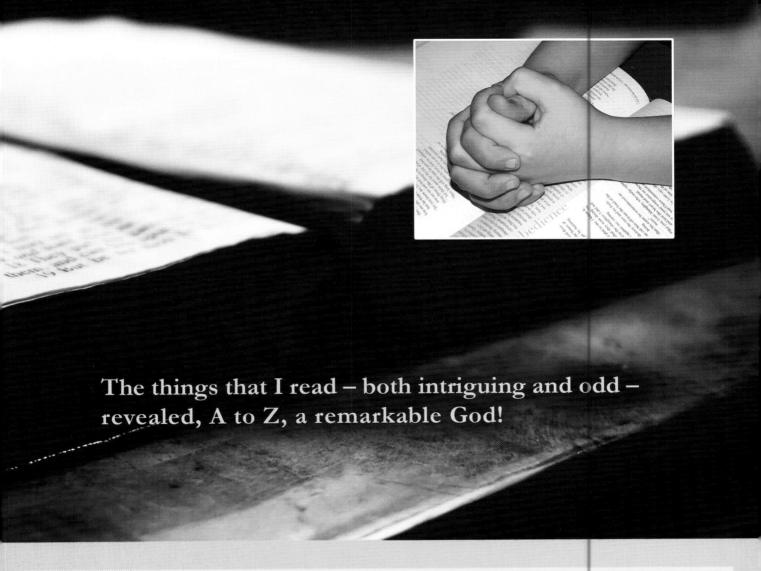

I read it for hours, day after day,
so hungry to see just what God had to say.
And each time I read it, I learned something new;
things that my mind had to ponder and chew.

The things that I read – both intriguing and odd –
revealed, A to Z, a remarkable God!

Talk to God — *"God, as I read the Bible to discover who You are, I know I will need Your help to understand it. But since You went to all the trouble of inspiring people from long ago to write down Your words, then it makes sense that You also would like to make those words come alive in my heart and mind. So, God, please give me wisdom and insight as I read each verse so that I can know what You are really saying."*

Thank God for preserving His Word for all these years so that your Maker can so clearly reveal Himself to you.

God is... Almighty

"I am the Alpha and the Omega," says the Lord God,
"the One who is and who was and who is to come, the Almighty."
— Revelation 1:8

Ah Lord God! You have made the heavens and the earth
by Your awesome power and by Your outstretched arm!
Nothing is too difficult for You...
— Jeremiah 32:17

I know that You can do all things,
and that no purpose or plan
of Yours can be thwarted.
— Job 42:2

A Closer Look — If you say that God is "awesome" or "amazing," you would certainly be correct. But you might also say "this video game is awesome" or "that pizza was amazing." These words don't go far enough in describing God. Many times in the Bible, God told people, "I am God Almighty" ("El Shaddai" in Hebrew). No problem is too hard for God because He is **omnipotent** (*omni* means "all" and *potent* means "powerful"). Many people in the Bible faced situations that looked impossible, unsolvable, and hopeless. The very same God that helped Moses (Exodus 14:5-31), King Jehoshaphat (2 Chronicles 20: 1-30), and a poor widow and her son (1 Kings 17:1-24) is able to help you, too. The Almighty's power extends beyond the distant galaxies and holds together the tiniest particles of matter, so no problem that you bring to Him is too big or too small.

God is ALMIGHTY. What does this mean?
There's no greater power, seen or unseen.
Behind the whole universe, He is the cause,
the One who's behind all our natural laws.
All nature obeys Him; the oceans, the weather.
He rules over matter and holds it together.
All of man's powers stretched out to full length
can't even approach God's unlimited strength.
God has no peers, no threats to His throne.
God stands supreme in a league of His own.

Our God is in His heaven;
He does whatever He pleases.
— Psalm 115:3

With God, nothing is impossible.
— Luke 1:37

Talk to God — *"Lord, I know that You are all-powerful, and that You are capable of doing things that are absolutely impossible for anyone else to do. Please remind me to ask You for help when I face difficult situations beyond my abilty. I believe what Ephesians 3:20 says, that You really can do far beyond what I could ever ask or imagine."*

Thank God for the displays of His mighty power that you have seen, and for things He has done on your behalf.

God is... Beautiful

One thing I have asked from the Lord; this I shall seek: that I may dwell in the house of the Lord all the days of my life, to behold the beauty of the Lord...
— Psalm 27:4

Splendor and majesty are in His presence. Strength and beauty are in His holy place.
— Psalm 96:6

B

Your eyes will behold your King in His beauty...
— Isaiah 33:17

A Closer Look — Who can deny the natural beauty of the world around us? If we watch very carefully, we may even get to see it unfold right before our eyes, like the glorious rising of the sun, or the opening of a flower's petals. The Master Artist is doing beautiful works in the hearts of His children, too. Although you may not always notice the progress He is making, you are one of His emerging masterpieces. Brushstroke by brushstroke, He is working on you. He promises that His people "will shine in His land like jewels in a crown — how lovely and beautiful they will be!" (Zechariah 9:16-17).

The BEAUTIFUL things that we hear and we see –
the song of a bird, a blossoming tree,
magnificent sunsets and colorful creatures,
faces of people with all kinds of features,
the laugh of a baby, a cloud floating by,
a babbling brook, a rare butterfly –
These great works of artistry sparkle like gems.
They start in God's heart, from where all beauty stems.
Our God fills His universe up to the brim
with breathtaking beauty, reflecting from Him.

I will meditate on the beauty of Your glorious majesty, and Your wonderful works.
– Psalm 145:5

On that day the Lord Almighty will appear as a beautiful crown...
– Isaiah 28:5

Talk to God – *"Lord, Your beautiful artistry is everywhere. Please remind me throughout my day to pause and notice Your handiwork. Open my eyes so that I may also see and appreciate the beautiful things that You are doing in my life and in the lives of those around me. I ask these things in the name of the One who is called 'Beautiful Savior', the Lord Jesus Christ."*

Thank Him for some of His finished masterpieces, and also for beautiful things He is in the process of doing.

God is... Creator

In the beginning God created the heavens and the earth. — Genesis 1:1

The fool says in his heart, "There is no God." — Psalm 14:1

...Let us kneel before the Lord our Maker. — Psalm 95:6

It is I who made the earth, and created man upon it. I stretched out the heavens with my hands. And I commanded the multitudes of stars. — Isaiah 45:12

A Closer Look — Even a casual glance at the natural world reveals obvious order and remarkable precision. The more carefully we explore our intricately designed universe — from our solar system to the mind-boggling complexities of DNA — the more apparent it becomes that a brilliant mastermind is behind it all. Sadly, some would rather give credit to some *un*intelligent force (or to life itself for "finding a way") than give thanks to the intelligent Creator who clearly reveals Himself to us in both nature and the Scriptures. The Bible rightly states that "it is He who has made us, and not we ourselves; we are His people..." (Psalm 100:3).

God is CREATOR of all that there is.
The credit and glory should only be His.
Every discovery scientists find
was formed by His hand and conceived in His mind.
Galaxies, animals, oceans and plants,
none were by accident; none were by chance.
Creatures with feathers, with scales, and with fur,
God merely spoke, and they suddenly were!
The mockers and scoffers who doubt their Creator
will have to acknowledge Him sooner or later.

*Through Him all things were made;
without Him nothing was made
that has been made.*
— John 1:3

Talk to God — *"Lord, I believe that You made all things out of nothing, and You are the Author of all life. I am amazed at the variety of things that You have designed and created, and at the way You have made my body — my eyes and ears, my bones and muscles, my brain and other organs — to function."*

Thank Him for creating you just the way He did. What unique features and characteristics has He given you? Acknowledge His wisdom regarding when, where, and how He placed you on this earth, and express your trust in Him regarding His plan and purpose for your life.

God is... Divine

How great You are, Sovereign Lord!
No one compares to You, and
there is no God but You...
— 2 Samuel 7:22

...There is no one like Me in all the earth.
— Exodus 9:14

A Closer Look — From the weakest to the strongest, every created being is dependent. Children need parents. Adults need each other. Animals depend on plants for survival, while plants require things like sunlight and water. But God is different. He needs nothing. The One who calls Himself "I AM" simply is (Exodus 3:14).

For thousands of years, mortals — who were created in God's image — have made "gods" in *their* image. Today, many people's minds still try to create their own versions of God. They want God to act like them (Psalm 50:21) and think like them (Isaiah 55:8-9), but He doesn't. He acts and thinks like God. That's because HE IS.

Do you not know? Have you not heard?
The Lord is the eternal God, the
Creator of the entire earth.
He will not grow tired or weary...
— Isaiah 40:28

There's no one like God. He's uniquely DIVINE.
His nature is totally different than mine.
There's one God alone, despite what men claim.
The "gods" they dream up aren't remotely the same.
No one sustains Him; He stands self-sufficient,
completely complete and in no way deficient.
There's nothing He lacks. He never runs short.
His being requires no outside support.
He doesn't grow weary and barely scrape by.
His source is Himself, and He'll never run dry.

His divine power has given us
everything we need for a godly life...
— 2 Peter 1:3

His unseen attributes, namely His eternal power and His divine nature,
have been clearly perceived ever since the creation of the world...
— Romans 1:20

Talk to God — *"Lord, I know that You don't need me for anything, but I need You for everything — every breath and every heartbeat of every day. I also need Your perspective and Your wisdom. I want to learn more about what You have to say about Yourself in Your Word, the Bible. In the name of Your Son Jesus, I ask that You would please teach me Your thoughts and Your ways. Amen."*

Thank Him for being who He is, the divine self-sufficient God who is all-sufficient for every one of your needs.

God is.... Eternal

Before the mountains were born, long before You made the world, from everlasting to everlasting you are God.
— Psalm 90:2

To the Lord a day is like a thousand years, and a thousand years is like a single day.
— 2 Peter 3:8

To the only God our Savior, through Jesus Christ our Lord, be glory, majesty, dominion and authority, before all time and now and forever.
— Jude 25

A Closer Look — It is hard to grasp the concept of timelessness. A book has a first page and a last page. Movies have opening and closing scenes. Baby birds hatch, then eventually die. We understand starting lines and finish lines, but a God with no beginning and no end is unlike anything else we are familiar with. Of course, we can know something to be true without fully understanding it. For example, scientists are certain about gravity and its effects, yet they can't truly understand it. It is mysterious, just like God's timelessness. Every created thing had a cause that came before it. But God was not created; no "cause" came before Him. In Heaven He is called the One "who was, who is, and who is to come....who lives forever and ever" (Revelation 4:8-9).

The eternal God is our hiding place; and underneath are His everlasting arms. — Deuteronomy 33:27

As I watched, thrones were set in place, and the Ancient of Days took His seat... — Daniel 7:9

...Give glory, honor, and thanks to Him who sits on the throne, who lives forever and ever... — Revelation 4:9

Your throne, O God, is forever and ever... — Hebrews 1:8

Before the stars twinkled, before the earth yawned,
before the first glimmer of light ever dawned,
unknown and alone, unmade, unassisted,
God the ETERNAL already existed.
Imagine the future through billions of years…
trillions…quadrillions…till time disappears.
God will keep living forever and ever.
When will He cease? The answer is never.
The best human minds cannot comprehend
how God remains God on and on without end.

Talk to God — *"My limited mind is finite, Lord, and I cannot grasp the idea of eternity. Yet I know that You have always been and You always will be, and that Your kingdom will last forever. In comparison, my life on this earth is relatively short. Please help me, God, to make daily choices with eternity in mind. I want to live my life in a way that makes a lasting difference in the lives of others. In the name of Jesus I pray, amen."*

Thank Him for thinking of you long before your were born, and that you can look to Him in the future, for all time and beyond.

God is... Faithful

*I will sing of the Lord's lovingkindness forever. With my mouth
I will make known Your faithfulness to all generations...
Your faithfulness surrounds You.*
— Psalm 89:1,8

*Let us hold tightly our confession of hope without wavering,
for He who promised is faithful.* — Hebrews 10:23

*Faithful is the One who calls you, and
He will most certainly bring it to pass.*
— 1 Thessalonians 5:24

A Closer Look — Have you ever been disappointed by people who didn't keep their word, or a business that refused to honor its guarantee? In truth, most of us would admit that we, too, have let people down. Maybe that's why this particular attribute of God is so attractive. God doesn't develop amnesia about His vows, or blow off His promises, or grow bored with His commitments. **Faithful** is one of His names (Revelation 19:11). Even in dark and cold seasons when we feel forgotten, "God is not a human that He should lie, or a mortal that He should go back on His word. Does He speak and then not act? Does He promise and not follow through?" (Numbers 23:19). When He begins a work in you, He will be faithful to see it to the end (Philippians 1:6).

The Lord's faithful kindness to us never ceases. His compassions never fail. They are new every morning. Great is Your faithfulness, O Lord! — Lamentations 3:22-23

God can be counted on. Maybe you've heard—
He sticks by His people and honors His Word.
FAITHFUL He is. What He says He will do.
He'll finish the good work He started in you.
He is the ultimate trustworthy friend,
my Father on whom I completely depend.
Men break commitments; their words can be cheap,
but God makes no promises He doesn't keep.
When leaning on God, your life is secure.
Whatever you face, you can trust Him for sure.

Talk to God — *"God, You are a Father that I can count on...a faithful friend. I know that You don't make Your promises lightly, and that You always honor Your Word. Help me to lean more heavily on You."*

An old song says:
"Count your many blessings; name them one by one,
And it will surprise you what the Lord has done."

Thank Him for ways He has been faithful to you. Make a list and be surprised at what the Lord has done!

God is... Good

...how much more will your heavenly Father give what is good to those who ask Him! — Matthew 7:11

And God saw everything He had made, and behold, it was very good. — Genesis 1:31

A Closer Look — When you're directly beneath a storm cloud, it's easy to forget that the sun still blazes high above. But who would blame the sun for the storm? The warmth of the sun is the very thing you long to feel again. It isn't easy to notice God's goodness while being drenched with pain and sorrow. But even in times of trouble that don't make sense to us, God, by His very nature, remains good. Countless blessings surround us in this life, and looking for them can help ease our way. And even as darkness closes in, God has a new dawn of glorious surprises waiting for us. David, who knew deep grief, wrote, "Surely Your goodness and lovingkindness will follow me all the days of my life, and I will dwell in the house of the Lord forever" (Psalm 23:6).

Every good gift and every perfect gift is from above,
coming down from the Father of lights...
— James 1:17

...He did good, and gave us rain from heaven, and
fruitful seasons, filling our hearts with food and gladness.
— Acts 14:17

Oh, how I wish the whole world understood
that God is entirely, thoroughly GOOD.
Though falsely accused again and again,
as people blame God for the choices of men,
He keeps pouring kindnesses, deed after deed,
providing the basics of life that we need:
oxygen, nourishment, sunshine, and love.
Indeed, life itself is a gift from above.
Pausing to thank Him allows me to see
how great is His grace that's been showered on me.

Talk to God — *"When bad things happen that I don't understand, I will still try to acknowledge Your goodness, Lord. During my toughest times, every breath, every loved one, and every moment is a gift from You. I believe that many things that I dread in this life I will thank You for someday when I can see them from a new vantage point. Please help me, Lord, to keep trusting that You always have my best interests in mind."*

Thank Him for any of His good gifts that come to mind that might be easy to overlook or take for granted.

God is... Holy

Holy, holy, holy, is the Lord God Almighty, who was and is and is to come!
— Revelation 4:8

There is no one holy like the Lord; there is none besides You...
— 1 Samuel 2:2

As for God, His way is perfect, and His Word is flawless...
— Psalm 18:30

A Closer Look — The longer we think about God, and the deeper we look into His character, the more we observe another kind of beauty beyond what is seen with our natural eyes. The Bible refers to the "beauty of God's holiness" (2 Chronicles 20:21). In a vision, the prophet Isaiah caught a glimpse of God on His throne. Angels called out, "Holy! Holy! Holy is the Lord Almighty!" and Isaiah cried out, "Woe is me! I'm doomed, for I am impure!" (Isaiah 6:1-8). As we start to grasp how perfectly pure God is, we begin to see just how messed up our thoughts, our speech, and our actions really are. But the holy God reaches down to unholy people to offer a lifesaving solution: His Son, Jesus Christ, the holy Lamb of God. (Read John 1:29 and John 3:16-21.)

HOLY is God. He is holy alone.
He's perfectly pure beyond all that is known.
There's no cleaner clean; there's no righter right.
In Him is no darkness, just dazzling light.
His crystal clear character keeps me in awe.
He hasn't the teeniest, tiniest flaw.
And though I am tainted and tarnished by sin,
the Holy One calls me, inviting me in.
"Come and be clean," my heart hears Him say.
"My Son bore your sins and has washed them away."

...the Ancient of Days took His seat on His throne.
His clothing was white as snow, and the hair on His head
like the purest wool; His throne was like flaming fire...
— Daniel 7:9

Christ brought you back to God
by His physical death, to present
you to Him holy and blameless...
— Colossians 1:22

Talk to God — *"Perfect. Pure. Holy. That's You, God. This world has been so tainted by sin that it barely resembles the paradise You created. That goes for me, too. I am imperfect, impure, and unholy. I could never get clean by myself. I need You to wash me thoroughly through Your Son Jesus."*

Thank Him for not leaving us in our messed up condition, and for offering the free gift of His Son, Jesus Christ, who washes away our sins and makes those who cling to Him holy, pure, and blameless in God's sight.

God is... Invisible

Now unto the King eternal, immortal, invisible, the only wise God, be honor and glory for ever and ever. Amen.
— 1 Timothy 1:17

Christ is the image of the invisible God,
the firstborn over all creation.
— Colossians 1:15

A Closer Look — The universe contains things that cannot be seen, yet scientists are certain that they exist. We can't see air because the gas particles are spread far apart, allowing light to pass through them. Black holes in space are invisible because their strong gravitational pull won't let light escape. The Bible tells us that God is spirit (John 4:24). We can't see Him with our natural eyes, but we can see the effects of His existence all around us. While the physical things that our eyes can see are temporary, the unseen things are eternal (2 Corinthians 4:18). Jesus said, "Blessed are those who have not seen Me, yet believe anyway" (John 20:29).

From the creation of the world the invisible things of Him are clearly seen, being understood through the things that are made...
— Romans 1:20

No one has ever seen God, but the Son, who is one with God and in close relationship with the Father. He has shown us what God is like.
— John 1:18

It's easy to doubt what our eyes cannot see.
If we can't detect it, then how can it be?
Many insist they must view it or hear it.
But God is INVISIBLE. He is a spirit
Who cannot be seen with my natural eyes.
But I see His handiwork all through the skies.
Through people I see many deeds that He does.
I see Him in Scripture; I read it because
His Spirit speaks tenderly right to my core,
and each day I sense Him a little bit more.

Talk to God — *"Lord, how can You be so invisible and yet so obvious? Sometimes it seems like these eyes that have never seen You can't miss You. Your fingerprint is everywhere! I look forward to the day when I will see You face to face. In the meantime, please help the eternal things that are unseen become more and more real to me every day as I walk with You."*

Thank Him for making His activity visible to us, and for the promise that one day our faith will become sight.

God is... Just

Justice and righteousness are Your throne's foundation...
— Psalm 89:14

"...As I (Jesus Christ) hear,
I judge, and My judgment is just,
for I seek not My own will
but the will of the Father
who sent Me."
— John 5:30

A Closer Look — Do you know anyone who studied extremely hard, but still got a lower grade than someone who didn't study at all? Or did you ever get in trouble for something that someone else did? One of the hardest facts to swallow in life is that things aren't always fair. Over and over again, history shows that our efforts to stamp out injustice fall short. Some people never get what they deserve – whether good or bad – in this life. Be patient; nobody's final sentence or reward comes in this life. Only God knows the whole story, and possesses the wisdom to sort it all out. Revelation 20:11-13 is quite clear — God **always** gets the final say.

...The Lord is a God of justice.
Blessed are all who wait for Him!
— Isaiah 30:18

Some escape justice, it seems, for their acts.
But God has a courtroom and knows all the facts.
Our one Supreme Justice, Most Honored and Highest,
is always impartial, completely unbiased.
His rulings are righteous. His findings are fair.
Challenge His judgments? No, I wouldn't dare!
The ultimate court date when all is revealed
will render God's verdicts that can't be appealed.
When time's final episode settles like dust,
all will see clearly that God has been **JUST**.

The Lord executes justice and righteousness
for all who are oppressed.
— Psalm 103:6

Talk to God — *"Sometimes I judge people quickly...harshly...wrongly. I know that's not my job. Please help me to focus more on loving people and serving them, and leave the judgment to You. Help me to worry less about always defending myself and to trust You for justice on my behalf, the way Jesus did, in whose name I pray. Amen." (1 Peter 2:23)*

Thank Him for being both an impartial judge and a rewarder; for hearing your cries and being your defender.

God is... Knowing

He counts the number of the stars, and He calls them all by name. — Psalm 147:4

Even the very hairs of your head are all numbered. Do not be afraid... — Luke 12:7

...God is greater than our hearts, and He knows all things. — 1 John 3:20

How deep are the riches of God's wisdom and knowledge! How unsearchable are His decisions and His thoughts beyond our understanding! — Romans 1:33

He reveals the hidden things, and knows what is in the darkness... — Daniel 2:22

A Closer Look — How much is one trillion? To get an idea, imagine if you were fortunate enough to find a full time job that paid you $480 *per hour*. You could earn one million dollars a year ($1,000,000)! At that rate (not figuring interest), you would have to work for a thousand years to earn your first billion, and a million years to earn your first trillion! Scientists now estimate that the universe contains at least one trillion trillions of stars! (That's one septillion, or 1,000,000,000,000,000,000,000,000!) God's Word tells us that He knows every one of them by name. Why would we ever doubt God's knowledge or question His solutions to our problems, especially when He is so eager to find teachable hearts who are willing to listen and learn? (Jeremiah 33:3)

God is all-KNOWING. Imagine the thought!
He can't be surprised, instructed or taught.
He knows every fact that would fascinate men.
Omniscient, He knows every what, why, and when.
He names every star. He numbers our hairs.
He knows every burden; He knows, and He cares.
Those feelings you feel that you'd rather not share?
He's in on your secrets, completely aware.
He understands just what will help you succeed.
God never guesses – He knows what you need.

Talk to God — *"God, the magnitude of Your knowledge overwhelms me. Forgive me for ever thinking that I know better than what Your Word tells me. I am humbled, not just by what You know, but by the fact that You would care to share any of Your wisdom with me. Please make my heart teachable, in Jesus' name."*

Thank Him that He knows what you need, and that He has the answer to every dilemma you face. Thank Him for His written Word, and invite Him to teach you His ways through it as you read it each day.

God is... Love

Whoever doesn't love doesn't know God, because God is love.
— 1 John 4:8

What amazing love the Father has lavished on us, that we should be called children of God!
— 1 John 3:1

Greater love has no one than this: that he lay down his life for his friends.
— John 15:13

May you know the love of Christ, which goes far beyond comprehension.
— Ephesians 3:19

We love because He first loved us.
— 1 John 4:19

A Closer Look — Everyone wants to be loved by someone. Maybe that's what makes us easy prey for "love scammers" — people who shower us with flowery words or maybe exorbitant gifts. It can feel and look so good for a while, but the underlying motivation is revealed eventually...usually accompanied by injury. Real love gives for the sake of giving; it doesn't manipulate emotions for the sake of taking. The Bible says that some people might lovingly sacrifice their lives to save someone noble or deserving. But God shows the true nature of His love by sending His Son, Jesus Christ, to die for us while we were still in a sinful and undeserving state (Romans 5:8). There was no hidden selfishness; He just loved us, pure and simple.

God so loved the world, that He gave His only Son, that whoever believes in Him should not perish, but have eternal life.
— *John 3:16*

...God proves His great love for us in that while we were still sinners, Christ died for us.
— *Romans 5:8*

From border to boundary, seashore to coast,
LOVE is what everyone's craving the most.
They search and they search, but often in vain.
They're offered a counterfeit, ending in pain.
Genuine love only comes from above.
The ultimate love giver — God *is* true love.
Not fleeting or selfish, and not superficial,
Christ's love lasts forever; it's pure, sacrificial.
He poured out His life, with me at my worst.
No wonder I love Him, for He loved me first.

Talk to God — *"Lord, I find in You the strongest, purest, and most convincing love my heart could ever wish for. It is hard to understand the depth of love that would cause Jesus go to such great lengths for me. I love You now because You loved me first with a powerful, lifechanging love. Please fill me with that kind of love for others — people for whom You died to save."*

Thank Him often throughout your day for His incredible love. Thank Him for ways that He shows His love to you through other people.

God is... Merciful

Yet the Lord our God is merciful and forgiving, even though we have rebelled against Him.
— Daniel 9:9

You, O Lord, are a merciful and gracious God, slow to anger and abounding in lovingkindness.
— Psalm 86:15

Be merciful, just as your Father is merciful.
— Luke 6:36

A Closer Look — Have you ever seen a video of an animal that somehow got itself entangled in a fence, or maybe got its head stuck in a plastic container? A common emotion felt by many is compassion, or pity, for the helpless creature. Then they find themselves cheering for the hero who comes to the rescue and releases the poor thing. In the same way, we all find ourselves trapped by our own foolish decisions, careless choices, and sinful behaviors. The Bible says that God feels compassion and pity for us because He knows how weak we are (Psalm 103:13-14). When people who are sinking in horrible pits call to Him, He pulls them out (Psalm 40:1-2). David said, "I love the Lord because He heard my pleas for mercy" (Psalm 28:6).

At times when I stubbornly fail to obey,
great waves of guilt come and sweep me away.
Afraid and ashamed at the mess that I'm in,
I cry out for help and acknowledge my sin.
My **MERCIFUL** Father has pity on me,
and Jesus, His Son, pulls me out of the sea.
No matter how far I am swept from the beach,
no ocean's so big that God's mercy can't reach.
My "good" deeds can't save me; I'm counting on His.
Oh, what a merciful Savior He is!

Therefore, let us approach the throne of grace
confidently, so that we may receive mercy
and find grace to help us in our time of need.
— Hebrews 4:16

Not because of any righteous deeds that we have done, but according to His mercy He saved us...
— Titus 3:5

Talk to God — *"I could never pull myself out of the deep water I often find myself in. You are such a Savior — one who comes to my rescue when I call on You, not because I deserve it, but because I need it. Please help me to show mercy to others the way You so often have shown mercy to me. I want to be compassionate like You, my Lord."*

Thank Him for being such a compassionate, merciful God, ready and able to rescue all who call on Him.

God is... Near

Remember, I am with you always, even to the end of time.
— Matthew 28:20

I will never leave you, nor will I ever forsake you. *— Hebrews 13:5*

Where could I hide from Your Spirit or escape Your presence? If I rise to heaven, You are there; Even if I lie down in the depths, You are there, too.
— Psalm 139:7-8

A Closer Look — Even in a crowd a person can feel lonely. Unfamiliar territory, like a new school or a new job, can be worse than awkward — it can be terrifying! In any uncomfortable setting — whether you don't know a soul in the room, or you are literally all by yourself — it makes a huge difference when a friend shows up. You feel safer; a little more confident. God has been reassuring His children for centuries with these words: *"I am with you."* He said it to Isaac (Genesis 26:24), Jacob (Genesis 28:15), Moses (Exodus 3:12), Joshua (Joshua 1:9), and Paul (Acts 18:10). Jesus told His friends, "I'll always be with you" (Matthew 28:20). In prisons, courtrooms, deserts, mountains, lonely islands, dark valleys, fiery furnaces and more, God sticks with His kids.

I've hiked remote mountains and sad lonely valleys.
I've walked desert roads and some dangerous alleys,
and places no signal could get to my phone.
Still, never once was I ever alone.
Each journey I take, I know that I know
that God's always **NEAR** me wherever I go.
He's right there beside me in loss or in gain.
He joins in my joy and takes part in my pain.
Darkness may hover and bitter winds moan,
but God remains near, so I'm never alone.

Draw near to God, and
He will draw near to you.
— James 4:8

The Lord is near to all
who sincerely call out to Him.
— Psalm 145:18

Talk to God — *"Lord, I believe what David wrote in the Psalms: Where can I go from Your Spirit? Where could I go from Your presence? If I go up to the heavens, You are there. If I sink down to the lowest place, You are there. If I flew on the wings of the morning to the other side of the sea, even there Your hand will guide me, and Your right hand would hold on to me (Psalm 139:7-10)."*

Thank Him for being such an ever-present friend and helper no matter where you are.

God is... One

Hear , O Israel: The Lord our God, the Lord is one!
— Deuteronomy 6:4

And Jesus answered, "The first of all the commandments is, Hear, O Israel; The Lord our God is one Lord..."
— Mark 12:29

Jesus said... "Anyone who has seen me has seen the Father...
believe Me when I say that I am in the Father and the Father is in Me..."
— John 14:9-11

Go and make disciples of all nations, baptizing them
in the name of the Father, and in the name of the Son,
and in the name of the Holy Spirit.
— Matthew 28:19

A Closer Look — The Bible is the story of one God who clearly reveals Himself to us as the Father, the Son, and the Holy Spirit. It's definitely puzzling, but it's only one of many mysteries you would expect an infinite God to have! The Father sent His Son Jesus to save us by dying for us (1 John 4:14), and Jesus sent the Holy Spirit to help us by living in us (John 14: 17; 15:26). God shows Himself to mankind as three Persons, perfectly unified in one Divine Essence. The word "trinity" combines two words that mean "three" in "one". Nothing in nature can adequately illustrate this fascinating truth about God. He made us, then came in the flesh to rescue us, then came in the Spirit to indwell us. This is the God of the universe. This is the God of the Bible.

*May the grace of the Lord Jesus Christ,
and the love of God,
and the fellowship of the Holy Spirit,
be with you all.*
—2 Corinthians 13:14

Try out this math; it's confusing but fun.

I and My Father are one.
— John 10:30

God is three Persons, but yet He is ONE.
The Father, the Son, and the Spirit – these three
are one triune God. It's a puzzle to me.
Examples fall short, but I know that it's true.
Comprehend God? I can't say that I do.
He's God, after all, so He's hard to explain.
Just pondering Him really boggles my brain.
We know God the Father through Jesus His Son,
Who sends us His Spirit – the great Three in One!

Talk to God — *"Lord God, there is no way that I could ever fully understand You, but I'm so glad that You understand me. I need You as my Father. I need You, Jesus, as my Savior. I need You Holy Spirit as my Guide. With all that I am, I embrace all that You are."*

Thank Him that you are no mystery to Him. Thank Him for being such a good and loving Father, a wonderful Savior and Friend, and a powerful Helper and Guide in your life.

God is... Patient

*The Lord longs to be gracious to you, so He is waiting,
that He may show you compassion...*
— Isaiah 30:18

*Return to the Lord your God, for He is gracious and
compassionate, slow to anger, and eager to forgive...*
— Joel 2:13

*The Lord is not slow to keep His promise, as some think.
He is patient for your sake, not wishing for any to perish,
but that all would come to repentance.*
— 2 Peter 3:9

*Keep in mind that the patience of the Lord
gives more people time to be saved.*
— 2 Peter 3:15

A Closer Look — Whether you're standing in a long line, waiting for a phone call, or counting down the days until your birthday, being patient is not an easy thing. Being patient with others can be particularly difficult. We might even get impatient with God when He doesn't seem to be answering our prayers as fast as we'd like. But if there is anyone who deserves to be waited for patiently, it is God. No one in all of history has ever shown more patience. For thousands of years He has waited for people, offering countless opportunities for them to listen to Him, to heed His warnings and follows His directions. The next time you feel tempted to be impatient with God, you might want to ask yourself this: Is it possible that He might be waiting for me?

I sometimes feel restless and very concerned.
I wonder, by now shouldn't Christ have returned?
This world seems so lost and so hopelessly wrong
that sometimes I ask, "God, what's taking so long?"
But God is so PATIENT. He wants to prevent
the loss of poor souls who still need to repent.
Just like for Noah, the sky's growing dark,
while God calls the lost to step into the ark.
And that's why, despite people's mocking and hating,
God just keeps calling…and patiently waiting.

*The Lord is patient
and abundant in mercy…*
— Numbers 14:18

Talk to God — *"Time and time again, You have been so incredibly patient with me, God. Forgive me when I get impatient with others, and especially when I'm feeling impatient toward You. I know that I can rest in the fact that You know precisely what You are doing. Teach me to wait on You, in Jesus' name."*

Thank Him for patiently waiting for you to turn to Him, long before you had ever given Him a thought. Thank Him for patiently working on you to grow the fruit of patience in your life.

God is... Quick

"He got up and returned to his father. But while he was still a long way off, his father saw him, and feeling great compassion for him ran to his son, threw his arms around his neck and kissed him."
— Luke 15:20

May Your mercy come quickly to meet us, Lord, for we need You so desperately.
— Psalm 79:8

A Closer Look — Jesus told a fascinating story about a father whose son demanded his inheritance early, turning his back on his upbringing and leaving home on unpleasant terms. The young man made many poor choices, squandering all his money on unhealthy and unholy living, until he eventually found himself penniless, friendless, and homeless, eating with pigs just to keep from starving. One day, feeling desperate, he decided to go home and humbly offer himself to his father as a hired servant. You can read the story and his father's response in Luke 15:11-32. This parable gives us a picture of God, always watching, eager for even the faintest glimmer of a sign that His kids are returning home. Seeing them in the distance, He races to them like a flash of lightning!

Slow to get angry, but QUICK to forgive,
that's God's example of how we should live.
An old secret sin once made me feel sick.
I finally confessed, and WOW was God quick!
My prayer barely fell from the tip of my tongue
and God, quick as lightning, had already sprung.
He rushed to my heart as I hobbled His way.
He dashed to my soul without any delay.
He ran like the wind, not breaking His stride,
and welcomed me back with His arms open wide.

"For Thou, O Lord, art good,
and ready to forgive..."
– Psalm 86:5

"He sends out His orders to the world,
and His word flies swiftly!"
– Psalm 147:15

Talk to God — *"I have turned to my own way many times, Lord, yet You are so amazingly quick to forgive me. Not only do You immediately welcome me back, but You eagerly get busy cleaning me off, never smearing my nose in my filth and foolishness. What an incredible God You are! Please transform me into someone who also is quick to forgive, just like You are."*

Thank Him for running to you with loving, forgiving arms, and for teaching you the importance of forgiving as you have been forgiven (Ephesians 4:32).

God is...
Redemptive

... "Don't be afraid, for I have redeemed you.
I have called you by name, and you are Mine."
— Isaiah 43:1

He gave Himself to redeem us, paying the full price to free us from all evil, in order
to make us pure — a people who belong to Him and are eager to do what is right.
— Titus 2:14

A Closer Look — **Redemption** is when payment is made to free something from its bad situation. The redeemer buys it out of its current state to give it a fresh start. A builder might buy and old run-down building or a broken piece of furniture because he sees its value and potential. Then he gets busy repairing and restoring it to a like-new condition. That's God's line of work. He looks past our current condition and desires us anyway. After paying top dollar for us — the life of His Son — He gets busy. Like a skillful craftsman, He mends us and reinforces us and sands us and polishes us into a glorious state, both beautiful and useful. These verses tell more about the work God does in us: Psalm 103:4; Jeremiah 32:38-39; Ezekiel 36:26; Romans 12:2; Ephesians 4:22-24.

God is REDEMPTIVE. He didn't think twice
to pick up our pieces and pay the full price.
Christ our Redeemer is always reclaiming,
restoring, refreshing, rebuilding, renaming,
retrieving, remaking, reforming, redoing,
repairing, reshaping, recouping, renewing.
God specializes in people who've failed,
whose hope has dried up, whose last ship has sailed.
When others say no, our Redeemer says yes,
then works a great miracle out of our mess.

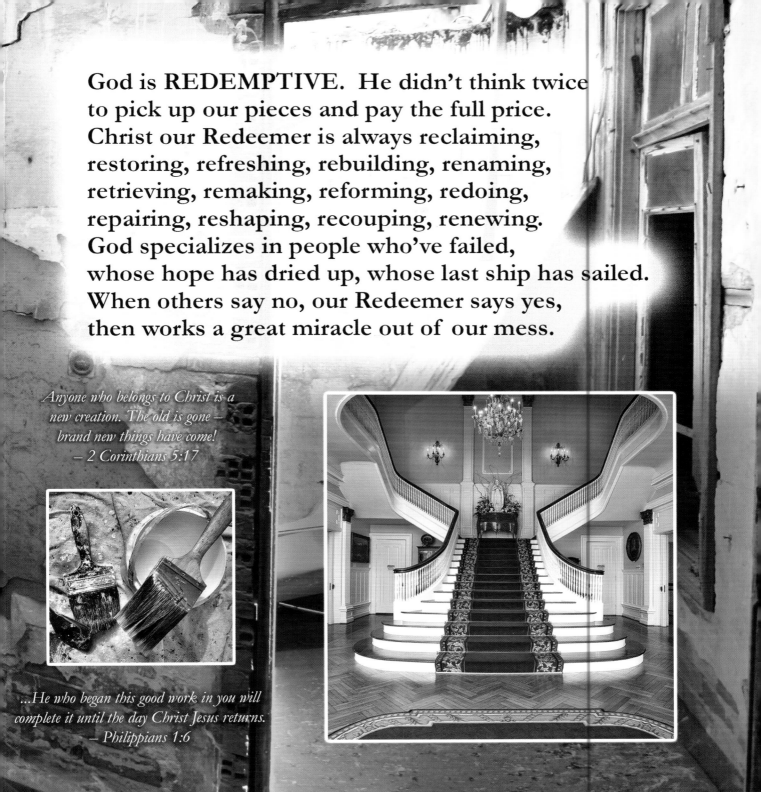

*Anyone who belongs to Christ is a
new creation. The old is gone —
brand new things have come!*
— 2 Corinthians 5:17

*...He who began this good work in you will
complete it until the day Christ Jesus returns.*
— Philippians 1:6

Talk to God — *"I had only one life to offer You, Lord, and it was a real mess. Why You would bother to purchase me, I may never understand, but You did. I know You're far from finished working on me, and I'm willing to accept all the repairs and revisions You think are necessary. I'm Your project now!"*

Thank Him for redeeming you, and for the beautiful transformation that He envisions for you. Thank Him that He is capable of doing things in your life that you never dared to dream would be possible.

God is... Sovereign

Your throne, O God, will last forever, and the scepter of Your kingdom is one of righteousness.
— Psalm 45:6

God has been our King since ancient times, working His salvation throughout the earth.
— Psalm 74:12

The Sovereign Lord comes with great might to rule with tremendous power. He will reward His people, and have their payment with Him.
— Isaiah 40:10

A Closer Look — For most of history (until the last 200 years), a common form of government was a **monarchy**, a word that means "one ruler." You probably know many stories about kings and queens even if you have not actually lived under the rule of one. Some kings and queens were selfish and cruel, while others tried to rule their people with fairness, though still imperfectly. Today, many countries look to a group of people to govern them, like a congress or a parliament. But God sits on a throne, not a committee. He is wise and just, so we can bow to His authority and obey Him with total confidence. We look forward to the glorious day when His everlasting kingdom will cover the whole earth. You can read about it in Revelation 21:1–22:5.

Millions refuse God the honor He's due.
They grumble, "No king's telling *me* what to do!"
But our God is SOVEREIGN, so He calls the shots.
Lesser kings often hatch self-serving plots,
and foolish kings selfishly do as they please,
but our King is noble in all His decrees.
He governs with wisdom, not on a whim,
for all of His subjects are precious to Him.
Someday, all people will worship and bow.
I choose to worship my Sovereign King now.

*Let all the kings
of the earth give
praise to You, Lord,
when they hear
what You decree.
May they sing of
the ways of the Lord,
for Your glory is so great.
— Psalm 138:4-5*

*...at the name of Jesus
every knee shall bow,
in heaven and on earth
and under the earth, and
every tongue confess that
Jesus Christ is Lord,
to the glory of
God the Father.
— Philippians 2:10-11*

Talk to God — *"God, I am happy to recognize You as my Sovereign King. Please forgive me when I am slow to obey, or when I go through the motions of obedience while not really bowing to You with my attitude. I have no right nor reason ever to rebel against You. You are worthy of my worship and my loyalty. Make my heart Your throne, my Lord, for I gladly crown You my King."*

Thank Him for ruling His people with righteousness, understanding, and compassion. Thank Him that His kingdom will last forever, and that all His subjects will be eternally blessed in it.

God is... True

"He is the Rock, and His work is perfect...a God of truth and without iniquity...
– Deuteronomy 32:4

God is not a man, that he should lie...has He spoken and will He not do it?
Has He promised and will He not make it good? – Numbers 23:19

...The testimony of the Lord is trustworthy...
the judgments of the Lord are true...
– Psalm 19:7, 9

A Closer Look — Precision is important to builders. They use tools to get accurate measurements, and to ensure that their walls are plumb and their floor are level. For centuries, those who navigated the seas have used instruments such as a compass to determine true north so they can arrive safely at their destination. Just as it would be unwise for a builder to trust what "feels" level, and for a sailor to set a course for what "feels" north, it would be foolish for us to build our lives or chart our futures merely by what "feels" right to us. Every word that God speaks is 100% trustworthy. Jesus told the Father, "Your Word is truth" (John 17:17), and said that we should live "by every word that comes from the mouth of God" (Matthew 4:4).

People may fool you. They lie and they bluff.
They try to deceive you with falsified fluff.
When words get so twisted, then what should you do?
Listen to God; He is totally TRUE.
Stand on His Word. It is firm like cement.
His nature is truth, one-hundred percent.
So, don't ever doubt any statement He makes,
for God cannot lie, and He makes no mistakes.
If truth is the thing that your mind truly seeks,
tune in to God; truth is all that He speaks.

*Jesus said, "I am the way, the truth and the life.
No one comes to the Father except through Me."
— John 14:6*

*...the hope of eternal life,
which God, who cannot lie,
promised before the world began...
— Titus 1:2*

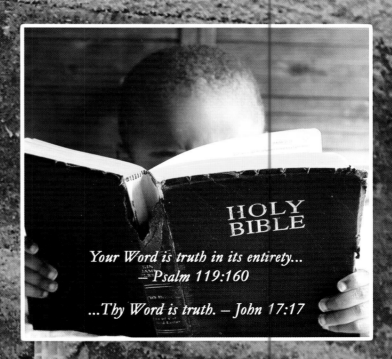

HOLY BIBLE

*Your Word is truth in its entirety...
— Psalm 119:160*

...Thy Word is truth. — John 17:17

Talk to God — *"Lord, there are so many voices out there that conflict with each other. Everyone seems to have their own version of 'truth.' I would be lost without You, Lord, my source of absolute truth. Help me to read Your Word faithfully to learn all that You have to teach me, for You will never steer me wrong."*

Thank Him for being reliable in all He says, and remaining true to all He is. Thank Him for giving us His written Word, the Bible, and His dear Son, Jesus, the living Word, who is the way, the truth, and the life.

God is... Unchanging

Jesus Christ is the same yesterday and today and forever. — Hebrews 13:8

We have this hope as a sure and steadfast anchor for the soul...
— Hebrew 6:19

God alone is my rock and my savior; He is my fortress, and I will not be shaken.
— Psalm 62:6

...He set my feet on a solid rock,
making me stand on secure ground.
— Psalm 40:2

A Closer Look — We live in a world of constant change from day to day, and sometimes from minute to minute. The stock market goes up and down. The weather can be hot one day and freezing the next. Couples who pledge undying love to each other might break up a week later. What medical journals might call bad for you this year may be hailed as a healthy choice next year. Opinions, moods, relationships, finances, strategies — the list goes on. It seems everything changes like shifting sand. Except God. He says, "I am the Lord, and I do not change" (Malachai 3:6). His nature, His character, His love, and His promises never alter; they never shift. "Forever, O Lord, Your Word is firmly settled in Heaven" (Psalm 119:89).

For I am the Lord, and I do not change...
— *Malachi 3:6*

You, O Lord, remain the same, and Your years will never end. — *Psalm 102:27*
...With the Father who created all celestial lights there is no variation or shifting shadow. — *James 1:17*

Like wind-shifted sand, like a wobbly table,
life can be fickle, unsteady, unstable.
Moods will swing one way, and then they'll swing back.
First you are cheered, then you're under attack.
On whom can you lean? That is easy to solve:
One who won't fluctuate, waver, evolve.
God is UNCHANGING. His viewpoint won't move.
His nature can't alter, reduce or improve.
That which He was He'll continue to be,
an anchor of constant assurance to me.

Talk to God — *"To me, Lord, You are like an immovable rock. I have been disappointed by people who didn't turn out to be who they appeared to be, and I'm sure I have disappointed others, too. But You are steady, continually demonstrating that You are all You claim to be. I know I can always lean on You."*

Thank Him for the confidence you have that God's love for you will never change, and for the assurance that He will remain constant throughout all other changes and seasons that life throws at you.

God is... Victorious

Thanks be to God, who gives us victory through our Lord Jesus Christ!
– 1 Corinthians 15:57

The horse is made ready for battle,
but victory belongs to the Lord.
– Proverbs 21:31

Their sword did not win the land,
nor did their arm bring them victory;
it was Your right hand, Your arm,
and the light of Your face...
– Psalm 44:3

A Closer Look — Only one team in the history of professional sports (baseball, football, basketball, and hockey) went undefeated for an entire season. The 1972 Miami Dolphins of the NFL won all 17 of their games... then proceeded to lose their second game the following season. No one always wins. George Washington, Napoleon Bonaparte, and Julius Caesar lost battles. Even those few generals who never lost on the battlefield eventually fell to one enemy: death. You might ask, "But didn't Jesus die?" Yes, He did, willingly and according to God's strategic plan. The difference is that He didn't stay in the grave! He says, "I am the living one who died, but look! I am alive forevermore, and I hold the keys of death and the grave" (Revelation 1:18).

In spite of God's goodness, He has many foes.
His wisdom they scoff at; His ways they oppose.
Yet, God warns the wicked to come to their senses.
Fighting with God has some real consequences.
Don't choose to join up with the forces of sin,
for God cannot lose and His foes cannot win.
They didn't defeat Him with hammer and nails.
Even in death, Jesus always prevails.
And when He arose, living and glorious,
God proved forever that He is VICTORIOUS.

God disarmed the spiritual powers and rulers, making them a public spectacle by triumphing over them on the cross.
— Colossians 2:15

Weep no more, for the Lion of the tribe of Judah, the Root of David, has triumphed! — Revelation 5:5

Talk to God — *"Many foes have always risen up against You, Lord God, to mock You and to try to silence Your gospel. Even at the end of the age when armies challenge You in battle, ultimate victory for You is certain. You have already defeated sin and death, and You have won my heart."*

Thank Him for leading you to victory over sin in your own life through faith in the Lord Jesus Christ. (1 John 5:4; 2 Corinthians 2:14; Romans 8:35-37)

God is...
Wonderful

The earth is in awe of Your wonders... — Psalm 65:8

Who is like You, radiant in holiness, magnificent in splendor, doing wonders?
— Exodus 15:11

Many, O Lord my God, are the wonders You have done, and Your thoughts toward us. No one can compare with You.
— Psalm 40:5

A Closer Look — Scientists estimate that we have explored only five percent of the ocean, and every year nearly 2,000 new species of marine life are added to our records. Seventy percent of our world's surface is covered by water, and the ocean's average depth is over two miles, the deepest part nearly seven miles! Truly, we have hardly begun to tap the ocean's wonders. Above the surface, on land and in the air are countless more breathtaking marvels. Still farther upward lie galaxies without number with unexplored splendors of their own. It is not surprising that David would write, "When I consider the works of Your hands...who is man that You should think of him; mere humans that You would care for them?" (Psalm 8:3-4).

From earth's lowest depths to the reaches of space,
God spreads His wonders all over the place.
The **WONDERFUL** eye-popping things that He does
prove God is a wonder if ever one was.
The most brilliant mind, informed and well-read,
God will leave speechless and scratching his head.
His wonderful wisdom I hunger to hear.
God speaks through His Word to my spiritual ear.
Sometimes He whispers and sometimes He thunders.
Oh, what a God of incredible wonders!

Great is the Lord, and worthy of the highest praise.
His greatness is incomprehensible. — Psalm 145:3

He does wonders that no one can fathom,
and marvels beyond number.
— Job 9:10

Talk to God — *"I cannot help but marvel, Lord, at the kind of wisdom, imagination, and power that could come up with such an awesome variety of wonders. When I add to that all Your miraculous, personal dealings with people, I am practically speechless. My heart agrees with the Psalm writer who said, 'O Lord, my Lord, how wonderful is Your name in all the earth!' (Psalm 8:1)."*

Thank Him for His astounding wonders that you have seen, the wonders you have not seen, and the mighty wonders He is yet to perform.

God is...
EXpressive

The Lord your God is with you...He will rejoice over you with loud shouts and exuberant singing. — Zephaniah 3:17

Hear Me, O My people, and I will warn you. If only you would listen to Me...! — Psalm 81:8

How I wish that My people would listen to Me... — Psalm 81:13

A Closer Look — It's hard for a friendship to stay strong if two people aren't speaking to each other. Misunderstandings are likely when neither person knows what the other is thinking or feeling. Our friendship with God is unique. He always understands our thoughts and feelings when we pray to Him, and He is eager to express His heart to us. In the Old Testament God spoke to His people through prophets who relayed God's words, which are carefully preserved for us. Today He speaks to us in an even more personal way — through His Son, Jesus (Hebrews 1:1-2), who told us more of what is in God's heart and how He feels about us. Then He sent His Holy Spirit to personally help us understand what His words mean to our lives (John 14:26).

Think God is passive and silent today?
No, He's **EXPRESSIVE** with plenty to say!
To those who will listen He gladly reveals
deep thoughts He is thinking and feelings He feels.
His Book of love letters will give you a clue
of how much He treasures and cherishes you.
So, read His expressions of love and affection.
Heed every caution and tender correction.
Be glad when He urgently sounds an alarm
expressing a warning to keep you from harm.

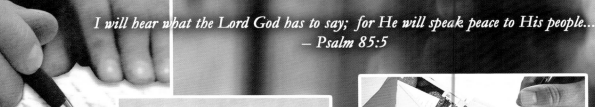

I will hear what the Lord God has to say; for He will speak peace to His people...
— Psalm 85:5

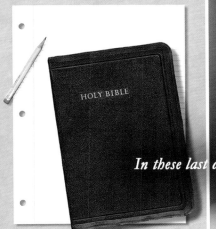

In these last days God has spoken to us by His Son...
— Hebrews 1:2

My sheep hear My voice... *— John 10:27*

Talk to God — *"Though my ears may not hear it, God, my spirit can hear my Shepherd's voice when I read Your Word and listen to the Holy Spirit explain it to my heart. I cherish our friendship, Lord, and I want to spend more time talking with You. Please help me make it more of a priority. Amen."*

Thank Him for the wonderful things He has to say to you through His love letter, the Bible. Thank Him for expressing His love to you through Jesus, and for sending His Spirit to guide you as you read His Word.

God is... Yearning

"...O how often I have longed to gather your children,
as a hen gathers her chicks under her wings!"
— Luke 13:34

The Lord will cover you with His feathers,
and you will be safe under His wings.
— Psalm 91:4

I revealed Myself to those who weren't seeking Me.
...To a people that didn't even pursue Me,
I said, "Here I am! Here I am!"
— Isaiah 65:1

A Closer Look — We all have longings, things that we yearn for. A girl may have her heart set on a horse, or a boy might very strongly wish for a puppy or a kitten. Some people long for a house of their very own. Others with high stress jobs often yearn for peace and quiet. Happiness, friendship, children, recognition, success, meaning...these are things that people yearn for. What does God yearn for? **You!** The Bible says that God's Spirit yearns for us intensely (James 4:5). Jesus longs to draw people to Himself like a hen gathers her chicks (Luke 13:34), and He deeply desires all people to come to know Him and be saved (1 Timothy 2:4).

The longer I serve Him, the more I am learning
that God is a God of unstoppable YEARNING.
He yearns to be with me; He's longing to spend
much time growing close like a friend with a friend.
He's yearning to lend His assistance for free.
He's yearning to share precious secrets with me.
For God wants relationship, potter with clay.
To think that He yearns for me blows me away.
"Lord, who am I that You'd give me a thought?"
"Someone," He says, "that I sought and I bought."

*Come to Me, all who are weary and troubled,
and I will give you rest. — Matthew 11:28*

*...The Lord is longing to be gracious to you;
He will rise up to show you compassion...
— Isaiah 30:18*

Talk to God — *"Lord, I agree with the Psalm writer who said, 'O God, You are my God; I earnestly search for You. My soul is thirsty for You. My entire self longs for You in a world that feels like a dry and weary land without water' (Psalm 63:1). I know that my desire for You springs out of the desire You feel toward me. I ask that You would always keep drawing me closer to You."*

Thank Him that, although He needs nothing, the Ruler of the universe yearns to be close to you.

God is... Zealous

...He wraps Himself in zeal as a cloak. — Isaiah 59:17

I will be zealous for My holy name. — Ezekiel 39:25

The Lord will advance like a champion. Like a mighty warrior He will stir up His zeal. With a loud shout He will raise the battle cry and triumph over His enemies. — Isaiah 42:13

The Lord will show zeal for His land, and have compassion on His people. — Joel 2:18

...The zeal of the Lord of Hosts will accomplish all this. — Isaiah 9:7

A Closer Look — The word "zeal" probably isn't one you use very often in your everyday speech. What does "zealous" mean? All sports fan want their teams to win, but some extremely avid fans root for their teams with a fervor and enthusiasm that makes everyone else seem apathetic by comparison. God is very passionate about some things. Jesus actually used a whip to drive out the sheep and cattle of greedy individuals who were commercializing God's temple and exploiting God's people (John 2:13-17). Today, instead of a physical building made of stone and brick, the "temple" where God dwells is His children (1 Corinthians 3:16; 6:19-20). The extreme length He has gone to reach us and reveal Himself to us shows just how zealous He is for us.

Bubbling, boiling, blazing like fire
deep in God's heart is a ZEALOUS desire
for evil to end, and for good to endure,
so all that He made once again will be pure.
Stirring in God is a mission, a passion,
to rescue the lost and to show them compassion.
The more that I seek Him, the more He seems real.
And that's why I'm starting to bubble with zeal
to love what He loves, to hear and obey,
zealous to follow each step of the way.

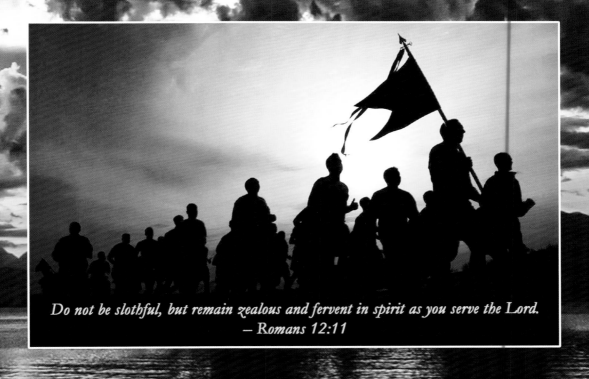

Do not be slothful, but remain zealous and fervent in spirit as you serve the Lord.
— Romans 12:11

Talk to God — *"The details of my life – my relationships, my responsibilities, my interests, my worries – they matter to me very much, Lord, but I know that You care even more about them than I do. Please give me a stronger passion – a greater zeal – for the things that matter to You. I want to serve You more enthusiastically and with a truer devotion, with all my heart, soul, mind, and strength. In the name of Jesus I pray, amen."*

Thank Him for not being apathetic about any of His creation, including you. Thank Him for the great zeal He has for your wellbeing, for the course your life takes, for your present situation, and for your eternal future.

By reading my Bible that sat on the shelf,
God showed me a glimpse – A to Z – of Himself.
And now I'm more eager than ever before
to know Him each day just a little bit more.

In Christ the full nature of God lives in human form.
– Colossians 2:9

A Final Thought

What kind of God would bother to create a masterpiece like you,
place you in a world like this, and not want to reveal Himself to you?
Of course He does! He is the
Almighty, **B**eautiful, **C**reative, **D**ivine, **E**ternal, **F**aithful, **G**ood, **H**oly,
Invisible, **J**ust, **K**nowing, **L**oving, **M**erciful, **N**ear, **O**ne, **P**atient, **Q**uick,
Redemptive, **S**overeign, **T**rue, **U**nchanging, **V**ictorious, **W**onderful,
E**X**pressive, **Y**earning, **Z**ealous God who reveals Himself to us in the Bible!

You will seek Me and find Me
when you search for Me
with all your heart.
— Jeremiah 29:13

A Closing Prayer

"God, the more I seek You, the more I discover who You really are,
and the more I discover, the more I love You.
Help me to keep seeking and finding as I search for You will all my heart.
I embrace You as my Heavenly Father.
I place my trust in You, Jesus, as my personal Savior and Lord.
I lean on You, Holy Spirit, as my intimate Helper and Guide.
I am Yours forever."

CHILDREN'S BOOKS *by* GARY BOWER

BOARD BOOKS

God Loves the World
God Paints the World
God Grows Our World
God Counts Our World
Mommy Love
Daddy Love

PICTURE BOOKS

Tessa's Treasures
Wyatt's Wagon
Ivy's Icicle
Cody's Castle
There's a Party In Heaven!
The Person I Marry
The Jingle in My Pocket
What Do Heroes Wear?
The Garden Where I Grow
The Beautiful Garden of Eden
A Patch on the Peak of Ararat
The Hurry-Up Exit from Egypt
The Frightening Philippi Jail
I'm a Michigan Kid!
Perfect Christmas
The ABCs of God
Away: *The Story of Jesus from Manger to Throne*

www.GaryBower.com